CREATIVE COUNTRY CRAFTS

ALISON JENKINS

CREATIVE COUNTRY CRAFTS

ALISON JENKINS

WITH AN INTRODUCTION
BY TESSA EVELEGH

COURAGE
BOOKS

AN IMPRINT OF RUNNING PRESS
PHILADELPHIA • LONDON

ISBN 1-56138-442-9

Library of Congress Cataloging-in-Publication Number 93-74694

This book was designed and produced by
Quintet Publishing Limited
6 Blundell Street
London N7 9BH

Creative Director: Richard Dewing
Designer: Isobel Gillan
Senior Editor: Laura Sandelson
Photographer: Paul Forrester

With thanks to Appalachia, the Folk Art Shop, for lending materials for photography and to Mavis Jenkins for working the sampler.

Typeset in Great Britain by
Central Southern Typesetters, Eastbourne
Manufactured in Singapore by Bright Arts Pte. Ltd.
Printed in Singapore by Star Standard Pte. Ltd.

First published by Courage Books

An imprint of Running Press Book Publishers
125 South Twenty-second Street
Philadelphia, Pennsylvania 19103

CONTENTS

THE CREATIVE CHARM
OF COUNTRY CRAFTS

NOTHING CAN BE more absorbing than the creative process. First, there is the vision of producing something beautiful and unique from what seems to be an unlikely pile of raw materials. Then as a form gradually begins to take shape, the mind can be emptied of all but minutiae, such as what color to choose next, or how long it will take to do the next section, in what amounts to a creative form of relaxation.

The key to trying out the traditional crafts ourselves does not mean looking back, shunning new ideas. Folk art never did stand still. It gradually metamorphosed over the years as each maker added a little of his or her personality into each successive piece. Today, we can benefit from a rich visual encyclopedia of shapes, colors, and forms, and tried-and-tested methods of working, while continuing to develop the craft, just as folk artists did in the past.

The danger we face nowadays when working on craft projects is the inclination to try to emulate the perfect finishes of factory-made products. This is a mistake. It is much better to forget the impersonal cloning of mass production and to understand that the aim of "perfection" is not only misplaced, but can stop us from even starting a project for fear that our work will not be "good" enough.

The Amish religion forbade intricate patchwork, lest it lead to pride. The resulting simple patchworks in surprisingly vibrant colors demonstrate the truth of "less is more."

In pre-Industrial Revolution days, everything had to be handmade. Perhaps folk then were less exacting judges of their handiwork, keeping the faultless for best, and letting the slightly less beautiful fulfill everyday needs. We also need to

This two-dimensional wooden chicken is inspired by the less common, though nonetheless authentic, traditional two-dimensional decoys. This one was made by Sally Lazar from North Carolina.

Garlands are traditional country decorations and can be made from almost anything. This arrangement, fashioned from gingerbread men, cranberries, and bay leaves, comes from Kentucky.

remember that, because communities had to make everything for themselves, they were doubtless more accomplished craftspeople. They learned their skills from an early age – girls had usually stitched their first rudimentary sampler by the time they were five – and by that age, Shetland Islanders in Scotland already knew the difference between knit and purl. Little wonder that Shetland handknits still have the reputation for being among the best in the world.

Nowadays, we expect instant excellence from ourselves. Disappointment at an early stage can mean we lay the tools of a craft aside for life after only one attempt. That is a shame, because very often the reason we feel we have "failed" is that we have tried to tackle too ambitious a first project. Simplicity has never lacked beauty. The Amish people of Pennsylvania demonstrated the magnificence of uncomplicated patchwork made with just a few pieces by juxtaposing solid colors that either quietly complemented each other, or sang out vibrantly

together. A successful first attempt offers great encouragement. Perfecting skills to produce ever more elaborate pieces is part of the enjoyment of craft work.

In centuries past, whenever people made things, they put a little of themselves into their work, improving their skills and developing their art form as they did so. The appeal is the unselfconscious way in which folk artists worked. Professional artists, who had studied, and were conscious of, contemporary artistic movements produced fine pieces, but their work sometimes lost its innocence along the way.

Folk art was open to everyone. Rich in imagery, it lent insight into peoples and their histories as it developed and matured. The visual arts were even more relevant in the centuries before the printed word was available to all than they are today. Messages had to be conveyed in motifs, many of which held a symbolism etched deep into the consciousness of the people. This, in its turn, led to a rich visual vocabulary – ready tools for folk design. Symbolic sun, moon, and stars, rooted in pagan times, are common to many cultures the world over. Layered upon these are the icons of all kinds of different religions, which traveled with peoples as they migrated across continents and oceans.

These delightful elephant dolls are dressed in traditional Shaker-style homespun fabric.

The folk art of North America from the 18th century holds particular fascination because it became a melting pot of cultures. Many groups came to America seeking religious freedom and for that reason kept themselves isolated. So influences rooted in one mother country became freed in another to develop in entirely different directions. A dramatic example of this is the contrast between the plain but brightly colored quilts produced by the Amish people, and the more flamboyant appliqué quilts worked by the Lutherans. Both were sects of reformed Christians from southern Germany and Switzerland. Other examples show a cross-filtration of ideas. Crafts borrowed from Native Americans were refined and adapted by settlers. Shaker baskets and decoy ducks both have roots in native traditions.

Without the benefits of a developed infrastructure comparable to those they left behind in Europe, settlers had to fall back on their own resources. There were not enough people for any but the most fundamental divisions of labor, so people tried their hand at whatever they could. Ministers and school-

masters would carefully script certificates; blacksmiths tried fashioning weathervanes; farmers carved decoy ducks; and tavern sign-painters branched out into portrait- or landscape-painting. Sometimes lacking the technical skills to emulate academic artists, these folk artists found easier ways to create the look they wanted. Motifs were simplified, outline shapes were cut from stencils, and molds were made to create form. Paintings were done to formulae, and illustrations used the strokes learned in calligraphy.

These are all tricks we can borrow from the past. So, if we lack the dexterity of an accomplished illustrator or an artist's natural gift of composition, we could cut a selection of stencils from motifs found in magazines and try out compositions before pencil ever needs to touch paper. That way, we could dispense with the worry of creating our own well-proportioned outlines or clever arrangements, while taking the opportunity to work on color, shading, and detail if we want.

Amish rag dolls were rarely given facial features, which were considered to make them too similar to pagan idols. These dolls were made by Cindi Hurlbut of Illinois.

Festive decorations were made from everyday materials threaded on to string or raffia. Here, bay leaves and cinnamon sticks join forces with corn on the cob and cranberries.

Color choices, in almost any medium, are probably the greatest deciding factor in the success of a project. This goes a long way toward the appeal of folk craft. Until the 20th century, most pigments used for paints, stains, and dyes came from natural sources, such as plants, flowers, and clays, creating sympathetic colors. Modern synthetic colors tend to be brasher, but coloring has become so sophisticated that endless subtle variations are now available. The trick is to draw inspiration from the shades of yesteryear, aiming for as close a match as possible using modern materials, which are often easier to handle.

The use of paints and other modern materials and equipment are perfectly legitimate in the tradition of folk art. Previous generations used whatever was available to them, so there is no reason why we should not use modern innovations to make life easier. If you can enlarge a motif to exactly the right size on a photocopier, why not do so? Or if iron-on fusible webbing holds an appliqué motif in place while you stitch, so much the better. This is the stuff of developing folk art. It is not about copying something that was done in the past – it is about drawing inspiration and adding our own touches.

This is the very spirit of this book. Insight into why and how particular crafts developed gives a deeper understanding of both the methods and the philosophies behind them.

The individually designed projects in the book, complete with instructions, are tasters to get you started. Each one is a testimony to the truth that handmade can be beautiful without being complicated. Enjoy gathering the materials you need for the project, and add style with color choices to suit your home – and make adaptations that offer space for your own creative expression.

MAKING THE USEFUL BEAUTIFUL

Artists – both fine and folk – have always dedicated themselves to the decorative, perfecting their skills and developing their creative expression on artifacts to be displayed and enjoyed as pieces of art. But what of everyday possessions? The utilitarian? The mundane?

Shaker Excellence

Day-to-day life becomes so much richer when we are surrounded by beautiful things. The most ordinary workaday items can be pleasing if they are well proportioned. The quest for efficiency often produces those elegant lines. The well-balanced basket that is easy to carry, the tool that has been perfectly weighted to make using it all the easier, have a natural harmony that is easy on the eye.

However, the discipline of discarding embellishment makes more demands on design and materials. There are no patterns or trims to disguise incongruous dimensions or rough components.

It was this quality in design that the Shaker community understood more than 100 years ago. "Don't make anything if it is not useful," their philosophy goes, "but if it is both useful and necessary, don't hesitate to make it beautiful as long as the decorative elements are an inherent part of the design and don't interfere with function." This wisdom, along with the particular and puritanical Shaker lifestyle, led to the design and making of exquisitely proportioned furniture and household items that were held up as paragons of quality in their time and are much sought today.

The Shakers' mixed but celibate communal living meant that there were plenty of hands to deal with the chores and distracting minutiae of life, such as the paying of bills, cooking, and cleaning. They lived for the salvation and good of all, with no financial gain for anyone – so those in the workshops had the time for the steady pursuit of excellence without the burden of worrying about economic survival. Following the advice of their founder, Mother Ann Lee, they worked as if they had 1,000 years to live, and as if they knew they were to die to-morrow. Their satisfaction was a job well done for its own sake. Shakers saw their skills as gifts from God, "Put your hands to work and your hearts to God," exhorted Mother Ann – and so the making of anything became a spiritual experience.

Many Shaker pieces were refinements of the everyday items the founders had used for many years in their native England. A classic example is the wooden oval box, universally recognized as an icon of Shaker quality, which was based on a box design that had been made in Europe for over 100 years. The Shakers simply refined it to the elegant proportions that became their trademark. The body of the box was made of pliable quartersawn maple, shaped around a form, while the tops and bottoms were of more stable pine, which was less likely than maple to bow up and pull away from the sides in damp winter weather.

The fluted lip around this prettily punched wall sconce protects the candle flame from drafts. This handcrafted design in tin has been given an antique finish.

The characteristic finger-like joints, known as swallowtail projections, allowed the maple to swell and shrink with changes in temperature and humidity, so the box was less likely to buckle than if it had a straight joint. The Shakers elongated the swallowtails to more elegant proportions, and cut them with a knife instead of a saw to bevel their edges. They pinned them into place with perfect lines of tacks made from copper, which would not discolor the wood. This detailing was the epitome of the Shaker saying "Trifles make perfection, but perfection itself is no trifle."

Charming in its simplicity, this tin lantern was an efficient lamp. The sides protected the flame from drafts, while reflecting and magnifying the light.

The pattern for Shaker baskets was borrowed from another culture – the Algonquin Indians. Instead of weaving whole, unsplit lengths of willow in the way that Mother Ann Lee's native English craftspeople would have done, these indigenous Americans made splints of wood to create a flatter weave. The Shakers adapted the methods, creating elegant curved and domed designs from what was a rugged prototype. During the 18th and 19th centuries, the Shakers made an industry of basketmaking, supplying their handiwork throughout settled America. Their baskets are regarded today as among the finest splint baskets ever made.

Decorative Tinware

In the world outside the Shaker community, other groups of early American settlers also sought ways to make utility household items more attractive. However, without the benefits of communal living, there was less time for the meditative craftsmanship needed to produce near-perfect forms, so their methods were generally decorative.

One example of this was tinware, which became much more refined at the beginning of the 18th century, after Paul Revere perfected a way to roll sheet metal, producing a finer material than the spun or stamped variety. Wall sconces, trinket boxes, candle holders, and panels for food safes were all made from tin, and often simply but effectively decorated with patterns of punched holes using a hammer and nail punch. The designs ranged from the child-like simplicity of concentric circles, squares, and diamonds to more elaborate compositions incorporating motifs from the makers' European roots. Hearts, flowers, birds, and baskets were popular, sometimes produced in outline, sometimes given fill-in and texture with closely punched holes.

Other tinware, such as pitchers, coffeepots, trays, and canisters, was japanned to imitate oriental lacquerware. First, the piece was given a layer of dark paint, often black, but sometimes vermilion, which was then painted – either freehand or using stencils – with brightly colored birds, flowers and fruits. Family tin shops, known as whitesmiths (in contrast to their heavier-duty counterparts, blacksmiths, who dealt in sooty iron) were set up all along the Eastern seaboard. The pieces, which were generally made by the menfolk and decorated by the women, were sold to itinerant peddlers, who would ply their way southward in a round trip that could be up to 1,000 miles or more. Some enterprising whitesmiths would head south and set up shop for a few months to supply the peddlers for their return journey.

Weathervanes – Street Sculpture

Folk art also had a place outdoors, in the form of weathervanes. These were essential in the early days, when folk were more reliant on the weather and there were no official forecasts. Weathervanes were cut from metal or carved from wood in simple silhouette. Often made by the craftsmen who also made trade signs, they were soon elevated to the status of local sculpture, taking on more detailed form, and, in the case of wood, careful coloring in polychrome for protection.

The choice of image often reflected the use of the building. A farmer, for example, might have chosen a rooster, cow, or horse. In coastal settlements, mermaids, sea serpents, sailors, whales, and ships predominated. Indians were also popular, partly because their arrows made perfect pointers to the direction of the wind, and partly because in some country districts, they were used to indicate that the land had been bought from the local tribe, keeping away other bands who might have assumed the land was rightfully theirs.

A dapper black and white duck is Pennsylvanian S. R. White's interpretation of an authentic decoy. The charm lies in the unique quality of each bird. Even today, decoy ducks are still handmade.

Developing Decoys

Another form of folk art sculpture, popular even today, is decoy-making. But the tradition of these highly decorative works is rooted in the most basic need – hunting for food. The idea was borrowed from the indigenous natives, who discovered that birds of a feather do indeed flock together and can be lured within shooting range by craftily positioned models of their own kind. The original Native American versions, crudely made from heaps of mud and bunches of leaves, were surprisingly effective, but the settlers soon improved the prototypes by carving them into more believable shapes.

The style depended on the breed of the bird. Some small shore birds needed to be seen in full profile, so they were mounted on sticks, known as stickups, while waterbirds, such as ducks and geese, responded to floating decoys. At the other end of the scale, some decoys were more stylized, with fowl assembled from pieces of driftwood, string, and nails. Once carved, the decoys were often painted. Some were given hasty symbolic markings, and although these were usually found to attract the prey much better than the more lifelike models, many makers prided themselves on meticulously painting in every feather.

Decoy-making still has a great following. Because they are inspired by a rudimentary native idea instead of coming from European roots, many connoisseurs would go as far as to say they are the only true American Settler folk art form.

THE ART OF THE NEEDLE

The hours women spent working with needle and thread in centuries past resulted in the flowering of some of the most creative and fascinating works of folk art. These tell stories of the lives of their creators, giving us an insight into their philosophies. From a young age, girls had to learn all manner of stitchery, so they could make and mend clothes, linens, and bedding, and were able to mark everything with embroidered initials. Tedious hours at school, spent laboring over the perfecting of these skills, were rewarded later when they could be used creatively to work exquisite embroidery and bedding, in one of the few creative outlets of their hard-working lives.

Sampler Simplicity

The first piece of a girl's creative stitchery was likely to be a sampler – probably an alphabet, together with her name and a date – worked in cross-stitch on a piece of linen. Subsequent samplers would include simple unshaded motifs that reflected the fashions of the time. In the 18th century, samplers often had religious overtones. However, after the French Revolution, religious symbolism was banned in France, and French needle-women began to stitch more everyday objects into their work. Houses, animals, vases of flowers, and bowls of fruit began to appear, along with roosters and peacocks in French needlework pieces, which were usually given a border of stylized flowers or trellises.

As work from France spread abroad, it influenced needle-women in other countries, and these motifs began to appear in their samplers and other work. Generally, girls made up their own designs, choosing motifs, alphabets, and borders offered by the teacher, and then arranging them around their name, a date, or perhaps a verse from the Bible. Later in life, young women sometimes stitched samplers to commemorate an event such as a birth or betrothal.

The charm of these cross-stitched samplers is their child-like simplicity: the two-dimensional representational shapes; the sometimes quaint proportions; the insight lent by the chosen verses. Since it is the naïve quality of antique samplers that is the very essence of their appeal, it is not difficult to design your own. There are endless books that offer patterns for borders, alphabets, and motifs. Or you can incorporate your own motifs, drawing them first on graph paper.

Cream and white fabrics displayed quilters' skills to greatest effect. Intricate patterns were executed in tiny, handmade stitches.

Geometric Patchwork

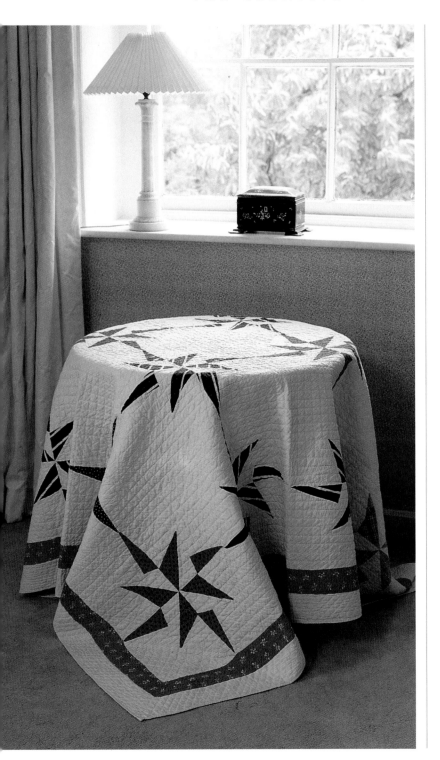

Quiltmaking is another testament to the importance of folk art. A thrifty means of nighttime protection against the winter cold, quilts also provide a record of an era: a little history, a little insight into a people was stitched into every top.

Quilts consist of three layers: a top; an insulating padding of wool or cotton batting (though nowadays, synthetic equivalents are often used); and a backing. All are topstitched together, either by hand with tiny running stitches, or, more recently, by machine. The stitching sometimes appears in straight lines, sometimes in intricate patterns. Generally, the plainer the quilt, the more elaborate the quilting, and vice versa. The tops are at once the most interesting and most beautiful part of a quilt. The sheer expense of fabrics in the days before mass production necessitated the stitching together of tiny scraps of fabric, gleaned from worn-out clothes and bedlinen, to make a rich patchwork cloth.

Patchwork was no innovation, even a few centuries ago. Paintings dating back to the time when Rameses III ruled Egypt, between 1200 and 1168 B.C., suggest the use of patchwork. But for centuries, it was seen as utility and, as the patchworks wore and disintegrated, so they were perhaps used as stuffing for the next quilt, leaving few early records. But when the idea of patchwork was introduced to North America by the English, probably around the early part of the 18th century, quilts were transformed into an art form. In Pennsylvania, especially, the German communities interpreted patchwork to suit their own, often religious, philosophies to stunning effect. Even the simplest one-patch quilts, with squares in carefully chosen colors arranged neatly side by side, could become an exquisite visual family history when made up of fabric scraps collected over generations.

More elaborate patchworks used a variety of different shapes – triangles, diamonds, hexagons, octagons, pentagons, arranged together to form blocks of patterns. These were given evocative names such as "Storm at Sea," "Mariner's Compass,"

A modern appliqué takes inspiration from the Shaker motto: "Hearts to God and Hands to Work."

"Flying Geese," "Bear's Tracks," and "Log Cabin," or the more religious "Crown of Thorns," "Joseph's Coat," and "Jacob's Ladder," witness both to the roots of each community and the tough lives the people led.

Once all the blocks needed to make the quilt had been completed, they were arranged in an overall design and stitched together. This offered ample opportunity for elaborate finished patchworks and made handling easier while work was in progress. The blocks may have been composed of four, five, six, or many more pieces. The more components in each block, the more accurate the cutting and stitching of each piece had to be; otherwise, the design became distorted at the outer edges. The supreme test of skill in patchworking was to tackle a patchwork that featured a large central block made of many pieces – such as a sunburst or a pieced star in which sometimes hundreds of tiny diamonds were meticulously cut out and carefully stitched together.

Curvaceous Appliqué

Many quilt tops were appliquéd: fabric motifs were stitched to a background cloth to make an elaborate overall design. Sometimes, appliqué was used on its own, but it was more often used in conjunction with patchwork. Appliqué allowed for a break from the strictly geometric patchwork designs favored by the stricter religious sects, giving room for more sensuous curving motifs – such as flowers, leaves, and hearts – that often harked back to European roots. Many of the motifs carried religious symbolism relevant to the more moderate reformed groups. To them, lilies were a symbol of purity and the Virgin Mary; flowers represented Christ; the Rose of Sharon alluded to the Old Testament Song of Solomon; and stars were often called "The Star of Bethlehem" or "Star of the East."

Amish Purity

In sharp contrast to this elaborate decoration, the early Amish people with their strictly puritan ideals shunned all forms of decoration, from the use of printed fabric (unless it was used as a backing, hidden from view) to any kind of appliqué with its curved forms. Even the use of too many pieces was frowned on, lest the finished piece become a source of pride. But these restraints have left us with a rich legacy of quilts of extraordinary beauty consisting of large squares, triangles, and rectangles in plain, though often bright, colors, all the more intensified by the popular use of a black background.

Closeted from the outside world, the Amish were not influenced by the current quilting fashions, so they had to rely on their own sense of design. With little to inspire them in their spartan homes, they resorted to everyday items for ideas. Some of the classic Amish designs bore a remarkable resemblance to the hymnals they brought from their German homelands, with square brass bosses in the corners and central brass diamonds.

As some groups of Amish began to move away, often to form less conservative religious communities, so their quilts became more vibrant. Heading west to Ohio, Indiana, Iowa, Illinois, and Missouri, they began to interact more with the outside world, and their quilts came to reflect this. The colors became more vibrant, the pieces smaller, and patterns and blocks were incorporated. Occasionally Amish women would even appliqué a central motif into their quilt, which would have been taboo back home.

While the piecing of an Amish quilt is traditionally very simple and usually done by machine to create perfect sharp corners, the quilting, which was done by hand, was among the most intricate found in America. They would aim for 20 stitches to the inch (almost impossible nowadays, if you use synthetic, rather than wool fillings), working the whole quilt in finely executed designs. It is interesting that these designs were often in the form of leaves, flowers, feathers, tulips, wreaths, stars, trellises, and baskets — motifs that were almost identical to those used for appliqué by the less puritanical Pennsylvanian sects. Bearing testimony to their European roots, the Amish perhaps justified this embellishment by using discreet matching threads for the quilting to keep the patterning subtle.

Quilting Detail

Common to many North Americans of any religious sect, quiltmaking became an important part of a girl's life from an early age. The skills were learned at school, and girls were expected to complete one cover a year, piecing the top over winter, ready for quilting in the spring. The finished article would then be put away in a hope chest, which usually contained 12 quilts. The 13th, which would be completed when she was about 21, was generally held to be the bridal quilt.

In North America, quilting was a communal job. Women would gather at a quilting bee and aim to have the cover stitched together by the end of the day. Even the children would lend a hand, threading needles for a penny a time. Quilting bees were often combined with a barn-raising (which the men would tackle), or some other celebration. When a girl invited friends to quilt her 13th cover (the bridal quilt), she was also inviting them to her engagement party.

The making of a whole quilt was often a communal effort. Sometimes each woman in the community would make a block to be sewn into what was known as an Album or Presentation quilt. This would be given as a gift to a bride or a respected member of the community such as a minister or a nurse. A young man might get a Freedom presentation quilt on his 21st

A contemporary one-patch quilt in coordinating prints demonstrates how simplicity can be inspired by the intricacies of yesteryear to great effect.

birthday, and a family moving away might be given a Friendship presentation quilt with each block signed by its maker, a former neighbor.

Such fast-track quilting probably had its roots in the early settler days when there was a great need to provide winter warmth in a hurry. In those days, quilts were used as underblankets and curtains as well as bedcovers, and many were needed for each family. Communal quilting certainly contrasted with the English practice. There, quilting was a craft to be carried out with pride by both men and women. Quilters either took work into their homes or traveled from farm to farm, staying on the premises until the job was done. They were jealous of their own personal styles and would not have wanted anyone to lend a hand.

A small cream bear, clutching a bag of cinnamon sticks, makes a charming gift.

TIME FOR TOYS

It is hard to imagine, given the hard work simply to survive in the last century, that there was any time left for making toys. But toymaking has always had a special place in traditional crafts, appealing both to children and to the child in the adult. Children prefer simplicity, often choosing the symbolic rather than the realistic, allowing space for their imagination. This lends a freedom to the makers – and it goes a long way to explaining the appeal of handmade toys. The uneven features on a doll's face simply add character.

Rag Dolls

Unless you are handy with a jigsaw and plane, probably the easiest toys to make at home are rag dolls. Little girls everywhere love their soft huggable bodies, and with their hand-stitched faces, each one has a personality of its own. Simple removable clothes add to the enjoyment for the child.

The most famous rag doll in recent history, Raggedy Ann, not only spawned a million lookalikes, but became the heroine of a series of children's books. Her story is a poignant one, that even today seems to bring her alive. The original Raggedy Ann must go back to the early part of the last century, because she was found in an attic in 1914 by her original owner's great-grand-daughter, Marcella Gruelle. Thrilled by her discovery, Marcella took the worn and faceless rag doll to her artist/writer father, Johnny, who revived it by sewing on two button eyes, drawing in a triangular nose, a smile, and a heart on her chest, under which he inscribed "I love you." Marcella named her Raggedy Ann after the characters in James's Whitcombe's poems – Raggedy Man and Orphan Annie. Sadly, Marcella died just three years later, but she will be remembered through the Raggedy Ann Stories which her father subsequently wrote and illustrated.

Wooden Toys

Folk rag dolls really only date back to the last century, because before that the cost of cloth made them prohibitively expensive. Earlier, most folk dolls and other toys were whittled from wood, a tradition that goes back to prehistory. Those early dolls were not playthings – they were often mystical figures used for religious purposes. However, there are references to dolls used as toys in early Greek and Roman literature. These had almost disappeared by medieval times – perhaps because children were expected to contribute their share of chores to the household and had no time for dolls. Perhaps, also, dolls were shunned by religious groups for being too like graven images. Certainly, until recently Amish girls had to make do with a stick or a bottle wrapped in a blanket for a doll. And even when the Amish did start to sew dolls, they were forbidden to sew features on their faces, which were left blank.

In Europe, the modern tradition for dollmaking dates back to 15th-century Nuremburg, which later became the toy-making center of the world. From 1700, dolls were carved in wood and painted in a style that was copied all over Europe and which influenced the German settlers in North America.

In 18th-century England, hand-carved and painted Queen Anne dolls became very popular. They were made both at home and by craftsmen. Each one had an individual, hand-made charm. This was not seen on the continent of Europe, where trades guilds dictated that carvers should pass the dolls on to specialist painters. Later, intricately jointed wooden peg dolls, also known as Dutch dolls (a corruption of Deutsch) were imported in their thousands from Germany. Their main feature, which has endured right up to the present day, is the painted-on, centrally parted black hair, a style typical of the mid-19th century.

A simple form of these dolls has been copied even by children, who used to paint the top knob of a wooden clothes-pin with facial features and the characteristic hairstyle and

This simple rag doll, complete with a huge heart on her chest, has been dressed in traditional Shaker homespun fabrics.

then dress the "doll" using fabric scraps. Records in an 1895 women's magazine show a slightly more elaborate and certainly more fashionable "Clothespin Doll," complete with full instructions on how to make elaborate crêpe-paper dresses trimmed with lace and tulle.

American checkerboards were often decorated with paintings, a tradition probably originated by tavern sign writers supplementing their income with smaller sidelines. This one, crackle glazed for antique effect, is made by Barbara Wagaman from Pennsylvania.

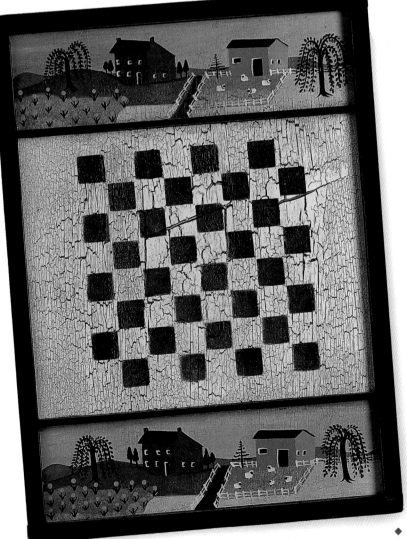

Ephemeral Toys

Dolls have always been made from whatever is around. Farm children may have made horticultural dolls – a magazine article from 1869 suggests making one from an upside-down hollyhock flower with straw arms, and a head of grapes topped with corn-silk hair.

Other ephemeral dolls, loved down the ages, are paper cutouts. These were sold on sheets along with cutout clothes. Victorian magazines exhorted children to make their own dolls from "Bristol Board" mounted on a wire stand and then gave patterns for elaborate frocks and hats. Sometimes it was suggested that adjustments be made to give the doll more lifelike proportions, so that women could use the dressed doll as a model for their dressmakers. This harks back to 18th-century France, when couturiers made life-size or half-size dolls, which were dressed in the latest samples and sent all around Europe to display the latest fashions. These were called "dolls of the Rue St Honoré," which was the Parisian dressmaking center. As paper and printing became cheaper toward the end of the 19th century, they were replaced by paper figures with printed paper costumes.

Moving Toys and Whirligigs

Toys that move have always been popular, and toymakers down the centuries have striven to introduce movement by jointing dolls' limbs and transforming them into puppets, by adding wheels, and by employing more complicated techniques. Whirligigs, which are a form of tabletop weathervane, are a fine example of this. Such toys fall into two categories: jointed dolls in many forms; and windmill types. The simplest ones, like weathervanes, simply have propeller-type arms that spin the figure as the wind blows. This developed into an art form as whirligigs became more complex – with propellers, gears, and rods that made figures ride bicycles, chop wood, or milk cows. They were often put in front of a house, on a fence, there to carry out their designated activity, gently or wildly depending on the weather. In religious communities, this was one toy allowed for the Sabbath, presumably to give time for meditation and contemplation.

Another toy allowed for the Sabbath was a Noah's Ark, because of its association with the Bible. This was fortunate, since wooden animals have always been a favorite theme for homemade toys. Most homes had a Noah's Ark complete with pairs of exotic animals from far-off lands copied from book illustrations. Sabbath was also the day that sailors and fishermen are thought to have made toys, many of which they whittled from whales' teeth, or scrimshaw as it was known.

Game Boards

In the days before radio and television, long evenings needed to be filled with games. Classic games like chess, backgammon, checkers, and tic-tac-toe, have been played for centuries in communities all around the world. Each area developed a different style of game board, often finely finished and painted or inlaid with ebony, ivory, or tooled leather.

In North America, game boards provided an opportunity for sign painters and hobby artists to display their skills. In addition to the simple checked design necessary for the play area, many were decorated with much more than a simple border design. Larger portions of the board – perhaps the top half, or a quarter above and a quarter below the squares – were given over to decorative space in which to place dispensed-with pieces during the game. The decoration could be anything from a few simple motifs to a stylized landscape typical of the painting style of the time, or a single image such as a rooster or a sunrise, similar to those that may have been seen on tavern signs. This gives rise to the idea that these decorative boards made useful sidelines for itinerant signwriters who were a little low on commissions.

Wire, twisted into heart shapes and attached to a wooden base, makes a delightful hanging basket.

The checked part of the design lends these simple but beautiful examples of folk art a graphic quality that is easy to reproduce authentically, yet the boards offer space for modern-day crafters to express themselves in their own style.

WELCOME HOME

From time immemorial, people the world over have wanted to make their home their own. It has never mattered how small or how temporary the home was – think of the cramped proportions of traditional gypsy caravans, which were, nevertheless, richly furnished with flamboyantly decorated artifacts and draped with elaborate fabrics; or the European barge folk,

who plied their ways around the canals of Europe in brightly decorated vessels, using tin utensils extravagantly painted in bright colors on black. The nomads of Arabia also had a rich tradition in their dwellings. Once the tents had been pitched on new desert sites, intricately designed rugs and carpets were laid out to make that place a home.

Somehow, the fewer resources there are around, the more resourceful people have to be. This was certainly true of the early American settlers, who brought very little with them from their European homelands, but carried in their imaginations all the visual influences they had left behind, which they tapped for ideas for decorating their new homes. Until consumer goods became readily available, generations of Americans had to rely on their own resources and skills to create all the necessities for living, along with any kind of decoration to enrich their lives.

Each group developed its own style, depending on religious beliefs and its members' homeland. The Shakers, whose leader, Mother Ann Lee, came from Manchester, England, espoused a devout belief that shunned all embellishment and developed the equivalent of modern minimalism. Furnishings were sparse; decoration absent. Without the distraction of pattern, focus was thrown onto form, providing a discipline of perfection.

The Pennsylvanian Germans also left their homelands for religious reasons. Some, like the Mennonites and the Amish, also shunned fancy decoration, though their style was far less monastic than that of the Shakers, allowing at least color, if not pattern. Other groups, like the Lutherans and other Reformed sects, came mainly from the weaving centers of Germany and Switzerland, bringing with them a rich visual dictionary which influenced the decoration of their homes, furniture, and textiles. This was overlaid with what they were able to accomplish, plus current influences being imported from Europe.

Whitesmiths fashioned tin into shapes, while the womenfolk painted them in bright shapes reminiscent of European bargeware.

Wall Stencils

Early American homes often had a simple charm, born of the fact that each community did not necessarily have skilled craftsmen of every type. As the communities became more established, there was time to add decoration in a style that has come to be seen as distinctly Pennsylvania Dutch. Their highly decorative, stenciled walls must be one of the most dramatic examples. Sometimes elaborate, sometimes simple designs in mellow reds, greens, and yellows were applied to backgrounds of plaster tinted white, pink, yellow, gray, light green, or light blue. The colors were hand-mixed using local clays and brick dust mixed with skimmed milk, creating tones that naturally sympathized with their surroundings.

The tradition for decorating walls is rooted in Europe of the 17th century, when a painter known as François of Rouen began to stencil lengths of paper to mimic the tapestries hanging in aristocratic French houses. The idea traveled to England, and on to the Bay Colony. Paper stainers used to stencil and later print patterns onto paper sheets measuring 22 by 32 inches/ 56 by 86 centimeters, though soon, 12-yard/11-meter lengths were sold on rolls.

However, by the time these costly papers had been shipped, they were prohibitively expensive for all but a few, so the idea of stenciling straight onto the walls was born. Itinerant bands of craftsmen would travel the area, decorating people's houses – and, at the same time, developing a folk art of their own. The intricate European designs proved to be too difficult and costly to reproduce, so the stencilers simplified the designs, further adding to their charm.

The arrangement of the stencils on the wall followed the conventions of wallpapering, with vertical bands of simple motifs separating panels of more complex designs. Very often, an elaborate focus design was applied over a mantelpiece, and borders were added at ceiling and baseboard level. The motifs were influenced by the original settlers' roots in southern Germany and Switzerland, so that they brought with them their own folk symbolism. Hearts and bells meant joy, pine-apples hospitality, and the willow, which was often seen in mourning pictures, symbolized immortality.

Floorings

Originally, floor-covering was no more than a rudimentary scattering of sand on boards, but as life became easier for the settlers, floorboards, like walls, were stenciled, usually with designs mimicking tiles or rugs. Alternatively, the boards were left plain and covered with colorfully decorated floorcloths made from canvas strengthened with linseed oil paint. Rag rugs were also used to "carpet" floorboards. As their name suggests, these were made from torn-up rags that were then either made into long plaits and coiled into a mat, or cut up and hooked into canvas for a looped rug effect.

Dower chests were typically decorated in panels, the number of panels depending on the size of the chest. German-style symbolic flowers in vases were a popular motif.

Overmantels and Fireboards

Sometimes, in place of a stenciled feature over the mantelpiece, a family would commission a painting. These were very often landscapes, usually painted by itinerant artists, who, while they were at it, may have painted the fireboard, too. Fireboards, used to seal off the fireplace in the summer, were wide wooden boards cut to fit the opening and held together with battens. It was commonplace to have them scenically decorated or painted with animals or vases of flowers.

Decorative Furniture

In country homes, furniture was painted, usually to disguise the plain softwood maple and pine it was made from. Sometimes, trompe l'oeil techniques were used to imitate the elegant hardwoods used by the English furnituremakers of the time, such as Hepplewhite and Sheraton. Techniques for applying color were developed, using sponges, rags, crumpled news-

Fruits and birds were typical subject matter of Victorian theorem paintings, which were executed using stencils carefully arranged into a pleasing composition. This modern one is by Hope Angier of Wiscasset, Maine.

papers, and feathers – a rich inheritance that is now enjoying renewed popularity.

Much more popular in 19th-century America was country furniture that had been colorfully painted and decorated. Simple cupboards, chests, chairs, tables, and even clocks were embellished with scripts and symbolic motifs rooted in the German homeland. Lilies symbolized the Madonna and purity; tulips, with their three upstanding petals, the Trinity; the half-fish Mermaid represented the half-human, half-divine Christ; and unicorns were considered the guardians of virginity. This type of decoration is still popular today.

Hope Chests

One of the richest sources of Pennsylvania folk art of this kind is found on hope chests, which were presented to women on the occasion of their betrothal, to hold the household linens, samplers, and quilts that would become their dowry. Some families made and decorated these themselves; others employed a local carpenter to make the chest, which was then painted by an itinerant decorator or Fractur artist who would have added names, dates, and inscriptions. Each region developed its own style. Lancaster County's distinctive look incorporated pale painted arched panels featuring elaborate motifs. The central panel often featured a male figure to represent the groom.

Popular Art

The walls of early American homes were hung with paintings of a distinctive style. Because they were usually painted by artists with little or no training, they did not display accurate proportions or perspectives, sophisticated compositions, or atmospheric lighting, but they had a naïve quality all their own. Full face portraits and landscapes were popular. Although few artists were trained, many were professional, in that they traveled around painting all manner of things – tavern and shop signs, portraits and landscapes, walls and furniture.

Ironically, many of the American folk painters who did have training were not professional, in the sense that they did not earn a living from their art. These were middle-class young ladies, who were sent to finishing school from about the 1830s to study, among other subjects, painting and composition.

It is indicative of the rigorous life in centuries past that it was considered an essential part of a young lady's education to learn how to make a Mourning Picture. These were often composed on velvet, using paint, needlework, scraps of fabric, and lace. Most included funeral motifs, such as mourners, willow trees, and urns, and often a church in the background.

A somewhat cheerier form of folk art was the Theorem Painting, which was made using stencils. It would probably be more accurate to call these compositions, as the women would cut their own stencils – often of extremely simple shapes such as fruits, trees, butterflies, and birds, and arrange them into a picture. The same shapes were used again and again to make different compositions. A good theorem painting showed skilled shading in the color and careful penning of details, executed once the colors had dried. It was a clever system that could produce excellent results, giving everyone the chance to make a beautiful picture.

CELEBRATIONS

Celebrations are the stuff of life's memories; the punctuation marks that highlight the special times against the humdrum background of life's routines. There is a basic human need, whatever our circumstances, to highlight our lives with festivities, annually commemorating the passing of the seasons, or marking the rites of passage – the birth of a baby, enrollment into adulthood, a marriage, a retirement. These days we still celebrate, but our greetings are sent on purchased cards; personal details recorded only on impersonal printed forms; and memories are stored in the family photograph album or on a video. In centuries past, heartfelt greetings and precious records all had to be executed by hand, and so were saved for the most special occasions and the dearest of friends and relatives, who treasured them as keepsakes.

Elegant Calligraphy

Beautifully scripted handwriting is admired nowadays as much, or maybe even more than it always was. But in the days before typewriters, even records and business correspondence had to be executed by hand, so good writing was paramount. Many hours were spent teaching children the art of calligraphy (literally "beautiful writing"), as a good hand was seen as a mark of education and culture.

In America during the 19th century, a schoolmaster, Platt Rogers Spencer, evolved a writing style that he had published as a manual for teaching penmanship in schools and business academies. Pupils learned a series of strokes – curved and straight, broad and fine, light and heavy – that were translated into the letters of the alphabet. This was taken a stage further by using those same strokes to create decorative illustrations.

Birds and animals were popular subjects for these drawings, because the use of calligraphic curves was an accomplished way of showing movement. A bold sweep across the page could become a bird in flight; finely traced flourishes the vanes of feathers. These illustrations were finished with a wash of watercolor and used to embellish writings. Sometimes, the illustrations and the script were worked on separate pieces of paper, to be cut out and arranged into an elegant composition on another sheet. Here, then, were the ingredients of greeting cards made and sent even by schoolchildren in the last century.

The Art of Fractur

Special documents, such as certificates of birth, baptism, or marriage deserved particular attention, and these were the occasions when, among the German-speaking communities, the Fractur artist would be employed. Fractur writing, a style of illuminated manuscript brought to America by German immigrants, was originally worked by members of religious communities. It had its roots in the handwritten illuminated works of medieval Europe and, by tradition, was rarely signed, so as to emulate the work of clerical scribes of centuries past.

Although Fractur was dying out in Europe, 19th-century America saw it flourishing into a folk art used to decorate all manner of things, as well as to illuminate documents, song books, and bookmarks. Hope chests and furniture, even walls were inscribed. And some of the stricter religious sects would commission Fractur to hang on the wall in place of portraits, which were prohibited by their faith. Church ministers and schoolmasters began to take on manuscript work, and as the demand grew, bands of itinerant Fractur artists would travel the land, accepting commissions for almost anything that could be commemorated, including family records or even a seasonal blessing.

Illuminated manuscripts, called Fractur, were used for all manner of certificates in 18th- and 19th-century Pennsylvania. This one, by Robert Miller from Maine, is made in the traditional manner.

Moving away from the original clerical influence, Fractur drawing and painting predictably grew more flamboyant and often less sophisticated because many of the artists were not trained. While early examples were finely executed and given subtle illustrative decoration with delicately colored illuminations, later ones showed more vibrantly toned illustrations that took up a greater and greater proportion of the work, in some cases replacing the script altogether.

Intricate Papercuts

Before the age of mass production, when greetings had to be handmade, even some of the less important celebrations, such as birthdays, Valentines, and seasonal festivities took on a more commemorative tone than they do today. If time and effort had to be put into making cards, there was sense in designing them to be kept, or even framed and hung on the wall. This is perhaps how paper-cutting developed from a simple childhood activity into a skill.

There is something beguiling about snipping simple shapes from folded paper which then opens into a pattern of perfect symmetry. This was transformed into an art form in 18th-century Switzerland, where black or white paper was scissored and scalpeled into intricate images incorporating delicate trellises, stylized trees with fine feathery leaves, urns, birds, animals, and flowers. In Poland, paper-cutting became a popular art, though the preference there was to build layer upon layer of papercuts into a collage, sometimes painting the motifs for extra depth. These traditions were transported to North America by the early settlers, who have left a legacy of finely cut and painted masterpieces.

The fascination for the fine cutting of paper could well have been fired by the late 18th-century/early 19th-century enthusiasm for silhouette-cutting. These profile portraits, originally cut from black paper, were popularized by those who could not afford to have a painted likeness. Silhouettes became such a craze in America by the 1820s that they spawned hundreds of professionals and thousands of amateurs, all of whom were extremely deft with scissors and paper.

Decking the Halls

Celebration has always called for the temporary decoration of homes in honor of the festivity. With no available ready-made ornamentation, the only option in the last century was to make use of everyday items and materials in what was often a more honest and sympathetic display. Arrangements of natural and often seasonal materials fitted happily into their surroundings, lending fragrant as well as decorative appeal. So at harvest time and Thanksgiving, freshly picked apples and pears offered a honeyed sweetness, while dried herbs and spices such as bay, cloves and cinnamon gave Christmas a pungent warmth.

Wire bent into various shapes, then threaded with cranberries and decorated with fir and fabric scraps, make original decorations.

From Elizabethan times, smaller fragrant decorations such as pomanders were popular. To make these, oranges were stuck with cloves and were preserved by allowing them to dry out slowly. When they were ready, they were arranged in bowls or hung on ribbons to be grouped into a display. The perfume was revived over the Christmas festivities with the occasional splashing of hot or boiling water.

Smaller festive decorations for hanging on trees and at windows were made from whatever was at hand. In Germany, many were cooked. Delicious biscuity *Lebkuchen* (life cakes), spiced with cinnamon and ginger, were cut into the shapes of stars, hearts, bells, and birds and threaded with ribbon for hanging, as were larger gingerbread hearts decorated with messages in icing. Salt dough was fashioned into simple and elaborate shapes, then glazed and baked so it could be kept for subsequent years. Elsewhere, simple shapes made from available materials, such as punched tin or fabric scraps, were popular. At other times, dried herbs and slices of dried fruits or vegetables were threaded onto wire forms. For Christmas, popular shapes were stars, bells, hearts, and angels, plus fish — an ancient Christian icon.

At Easter in many countries, it is traditional to decorate eggs, coloring them with natural dyes or using various techniques to pattern them. In Switzerland, young girls would tint eggs in glorious copper shades using a homemade dye prepared from onion skins. Sometimes they would make a mask using a spring leaf or flower before dyeing the egg so as to leave a seasonal imprint on the shell. The Swiss also engraved eggs, using a sharp knife to scratch a simple outline design of flora or fauna into the shell of a dyed egg.

In Poland and the Ukraine, the womenfolk used a batik method of wax-resist dyeing to produce intricately patterned eggs of many colors, all the more intensified by their traditionally black background. This art, known as Pisanki, traveled with immigrants to North America, where New England groups still make an annual ritual of elaborately decorating eggs in this way.

One of the less important celebrations, but one which is universally enjoyed, is St. Valentine's Day, when love tokens are secretly exchanged. Traditionally, all manner of cards were made – from intricate papercuts to collages of silk and lace. The "Heart in Hand," originally a religious symbol and indicative of love and piety, is sometimes used for Valentine cards. Some say the motif originates from the old English custom of a gentleman giving a glove to the woman of his choice on St. Valentine's Day.

A star-shaped Christmas decoration made in the same way as the heart shown opposite.

But whatever the past meanings, the Heart in Hand makes a symbolic Valentine card with an easy graphic shape that would look striking framed and hung on the wall . . . which, of course, continues the folk art tradition of keepsake cards.

MAKING THE USEFUL BEAUTIFUL

Shaker-style Bandbox

Rag Rug

Punched Tin Candle Sconces

Painted Tinware

Shaker-style Bandbox

*Oval boxes with a distinctive swallowtail joint have become a
signature of the style of the Shakers. This strict religious sect, an
offshoot of the Quakers, permitted little decoration in their homes, so
the beauty of these boxes lies in their functional simplicity. Boxes were
made in all sizes for storing anything and everything in the home.
Ladies traveling by stagecoach carried them as hand luggage. They
were originally fashioned from wood – traditionally maple and pine –
and were sometimes round, but oval is an easier shape to make.
In 18th-century England, bandboxes made from paper were popular
for storing gentlemen's shirt collars. These three oval stacking boxes
are made from cardboard and papier-mâché. They are useful for
storing small objects – earrings or keepsakes.*

1 Trace the templates (on page 34–5). Extend the side pieces by the appropriate measurements. Cut out the pattern pieces from cardboard.

MATERIALS AND EQUIPMENT

◆ large sheet of pliable craft cardboard

◆ a few sheets of newspaper

◆ masking tape

◆ double-sided tape

◆ craft knife

◆ metal ruler

◆ pencil

◆ gesso

◆ blue latex paint

◆ white glue

◆ 1 inch paintbrush

◆ awl

◆ small brass paper fasteners

◆ jar of wallpaper paste mixed to a thick soupy consistency

2 Bend the side pieces to fit tightly around the base and lid, making sure the swallowtail shape matches at the front. Hold the overlap in place with double-sided tape. Use masking tape to anchor the side pieces together on the inside.

3 Tear the sheets of newspaper into strips about 1¼–1½ inches wide. Coat the strips on both sides with wallpaper paste, then cover the cardboard box inside and outside with two or three layers. Smooth out any air bubbles with your fingers, then use your thumbnail to define the swallowtail shape. Leave the box in a warm place to dry completely.

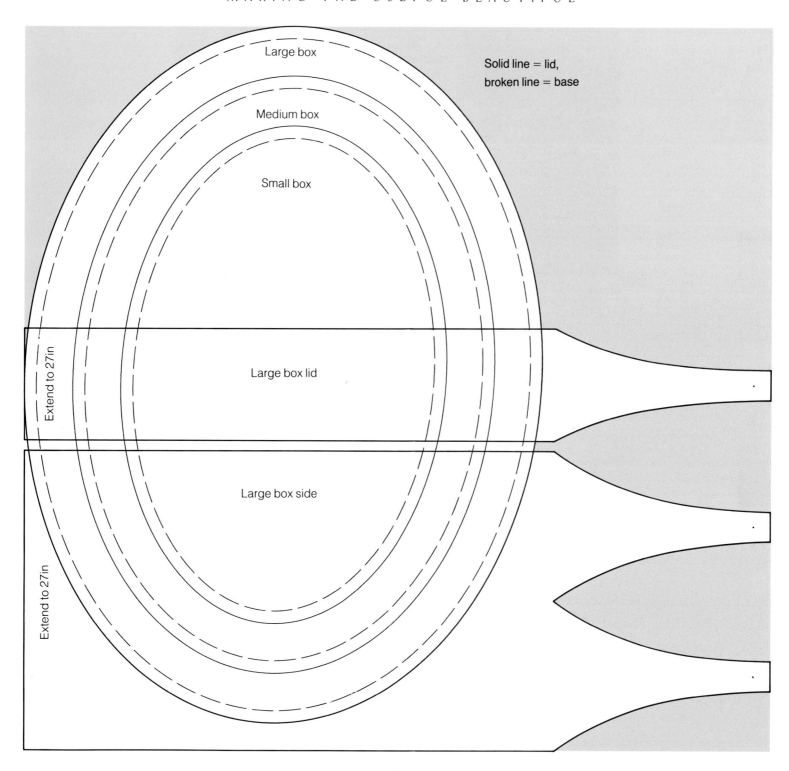

Large box

Medium box

Small box

Solid line = lid,
broken line = base

Extend to 27in

Large box lid

Large box side

Extend to 27in

Extend to 22in

Medium box lid

Extend to 22in

Medium box side

Extend to 18in

Small box lid

Extend to 18in

Small box side

4 Coat the box with gesso. This is a quick-drying acrylic paint used to seal the paper and to cover the newsprint.

TIP

Paint the inside of the box and lid in a contrasting color, or line with colored or patterned fabric.

5 Cover the outside of the box with one or two coats of blue latex paint. Allow a good drying time between coats. When the paint is dry, cover the paintwork with one coat of white glue to seal and protect the paint and to give a slight sheen.

6 Using an awl, pierce holes in the swallowtail overlaps where indicated on the pattern, and insert small brass paper fasteners. Open out the prongs of the fasteners on the inside.

Rag Rug

Weaving old bits of fabric together to make floor coverings was a way of making a home warmer and more comfortable in Europe for centuries. The craft traveled across the Atlantic with the first settlers in America – but because it was considered a working-class craft, not an art, it was dismissed, and its development went unrecorded.

We know, however, that rag rugs have been made by two main methods. Strips of fabric were tufted and prodded through a backing fabric or plaited into lengths and coiled in concentric circles. This colorful rug uses the last method. Make it from remnants of dress fabric, worn bedlinen or old, lightweight curtains. Plait or braid together strips of fabric, then stitch the plaits in a spiral, adding more plaits to make the rug the size you want.

1 Cut each fabric into strips about 2¾ inches wide. Join the strips together to make 6-foot lengths. Fold the raw edges to the centre, then use the safety pin to join the ends.

2 You will need to secure the safety pin to a hook or a nail in a wall or on your work surface. Plait or braid the fabric strips, folding in the raw edges as you go. Take care not to tangle the long ends of fabric.

MATERIALS AND EQUIPMENT

◆ cotton fabric in three colors or patterns

◆ sharp scissors

◆ matching sewing thread

◆ sewing needle

◆ large safety pin

3 When you reach the end, trim and baste two ends together, then wrap the third end around it to enclose the raw edges. Stitch neatly in place. Finish the other end in the same way.

4 To begin making the rug, coil a plait, and stitch each row to the previous one on the wrong side. Join on new plaits by stitching the finished ends into the folds of fabric and stitching securely in place. Add on as many plaits as you like.

TIPS

Plait three strips of fabric of the same color to add contrasting stripes or edging to your rug.

Sew on a fabric backing if the rug is to be used a lot.

Punched Tin Candle Sconces

German immigrants in Pennsylvania turned the new lightweight tin that became available during the 18th century to good use in their kitchens. Until then, cooking equipment was made from heavy iron, but the new rolled tin was strong, smooth, and light. Tinsmiths, called whitesmiths, fashioned sheets of tin into useful, lightweight kitchen implements – one whitesmith's line numbered 54 items. Thrifty homesteaders bought rolled tin and made things for themselves, turning a functional manufacturing process into a craft. Punched tinwork turned useful candle sconces – which protected the flames from drafts and reflected their light back into the room – into decorative objects. Make these pretty candle sconces by recycling tin cans, which are thin enough to be easy to cut and shape. The perforations that form the pattern are made by tapping a metal center punch into the tin. You can decorate old coffee cans with punched patterns. Just sand away any printing or paint, then punch in your design.

1 Remove the snap-on lid from the coffee can and cut the can in half with the tin snips. Cut off the base of the can and open out and flatten the side piece.

2 Trace and enlarge the pattern template. Cut out a basic sconce shape from the flattened tin sheet. Make small snips around the curved edge and bend back the little tabs you have formed using pliers. This will make the edge neat and safe.

MATERIALS AND EQUIPMENT

- large tin can (an empty coffee can)
- tin snips
- protective gloves
- tack hammer
- center punch
- pliers
- tracing paper
- pencil
- masking tape
- thick cardboard to protect your work surface
- small spring clips
- epoxy resin glue

Enlarge the template on a photocopier by 25%

Bend along dotted lines

3 Trim the edge of the pattern to fit the back of the sconce, and hold it in place with masking tape. Protect your work surface with a thick pad of cardboard.

4 Place the back of the sconce flat on the pad. Punch along the lines on the template using the center punch and a tack hammer.

5 Bend the lower edge over a piece of wood to form a right angle.

6 Glue the sconce back to the base using a strong epoxy resin. Hold it in place with a few small spring clips.

SAFETY NOTE

Always use protective gloves when handling cut metal, as the edges are very sharp.

TIPS

Old tin cans are a good source of material for sconces. Cut off the base and lid with tin snips or a can opener, then cut down the center seam and open out the side pieces.

Circular sconce

Use the base of the large can as a back for the circular candle sconce. Punch a heart motif at the center and around the base in concentric circles. Glue the back to a smaller can base to hold the candle.

Painted Tinware

*Transform plain tin tea caddies or canisters with hand-painted floral
motifs inspired by Pennsylvanian Dutch toleware. This colorful
tableware, made from sheet metal — usually tin — and painted,
enameled, or lacquered, was popular in the homes of German settlers
in Pennsylvania ("Dutch" is a corruption of "Deutsch"). Toleware was
decorative. Pitchers, coffeepots, trays, and containers were made to
give as presents on special occasions. They were kept and rarely used
except for decoration and display — which is why so many examples
have survived in beautiful condition to be displayed in museums today.
These brightly painted containers have a protective coating of varnish,
so they can be safely used and washed.*

1 Key the surface of the tea caddy with wet and dry sandpaper. Wipe it with a cloth soaked in mineral spirits to remove dust. Paint on two coats of matte black latex paint. Allow good drying time between coats, following the instructions on the paint tin. Trace the floral design. Tape the traced design to a piece of chalk-backed carbon paper of the same size, then transfer the design to the tin. Tape the carbon paper to the tin and trace through the layers with a pencil.

Pattern for lid

Pattern for side of tin

MATERIALS AND EQUIPMENT

- ◆ tin tea caddy
- ◆ tracing paper
- ◆ chalk-backed carbon paper
- ◆ pencil
- ◆ low tack masking tape
- ◆ wet and dry sandpaper
- ◆ small paintbrushes
- ◆ 1 inch paintbrush
- ◆ matte black latex paint
- ◆ acrylic paints (red, green, blue, yellow, white, and black)
- ◆ mixing palette
- ◆ clear varnish in a satin finish
- ◆ soft cloth and mineral spirits

2 Mix the basic base colors on a palette and apply them to each part of the design using a small paintbrush.

3 Lighten each color with white paint, then add details and highlights to the basic design. Use our picture as a guide, or experiment with your own ideas.

TIP

Acrylic paints are very quick-drying, and when dry they are permanent. They are ideal to use when you are handling the object you are painting, as they decrease the risk of smudging the design. Practice the brush strokes on a spare sheet of paper before decorating the tin to accustom yourself to the flowing motion required.

4 When the paint is dry, lightly wipe over with a soft cloth soaked in mineral spirits to remove the chalk marks. Apply two coats of clear satin varnish with a 1 inch paintbrush, allowing good drying time between coats.

THE ART OF THE NEEDLE

Pieced Patchwork Pillow

Pillows are a modern application of a traditional craft. The farmsteads of hardworking American settlers were furnished with objects that were largely functional. Quilts were used to cover beds and windows at cold times of year, not to make soft places to sit; and pillows were often the only cushions in a home.

But the patchwork squares from which quilt patterns are made up are an ideal size for modern throw pillows, and the traditional patchwork patterns make striking pillow covers. Many of the classic quilt patterns were based on religious themes – the red cover on the right uses a traditional pattern called "Cross and Crown," commemorating Jesus and the crown of thorns. The green pattern on the left is called "Evening Star."

MATERIALS AND EQUIPMENT

Cross and Crown Pillow

- ◆ 20 inches of 44-inch wide ivory fabric
- ◆ 12 inches of 44-inch wide red dotted cotton fabric
- ◆ 4 × 4-inch square red cotton fabric
- ◆ sewing needles and pins
- ◆ matching sewing thread
- ◆ sharp scissors
- ◆ sheet of plain pattern paper
- ◆ pencil and ruler
- ◆ 14-inch square pillow form

Note: this cover fits a 14-inch pillow form. Adjust pattern and fabric requirements accordingly if your form is larger or smaller.

DRAFTING THE PATTERN

You will see from the patchwork diagram that the 14-inch square pattern is divided into five equal parts along each side to form a grid of 25 squares. The squares can then be joined, divided or subdivided to form the pattern.

Most patchwork designs are made from squares with sides divided into 4, 5, 7 or 9 equal parts, and are thus called 4, 5, 7 or 9 "patch" designs. The variations are limitless, so why not use a traditional design as an inspiration to create your own patchwork using a blank grid?

1 Draw the pattern full size on a plain sheet of paper, cut out the basic pieces, numbers 1, 2, 3, and 4. Redraw these pieces, adding ⅝-inch seam allowance all around. Number the pattern pieces as indicated.

2 For the pillow backs, draw on plain paper a rectangle two-thirds the depth of the pillow front, add ⅝-inch seam allowance all around.

Patch grid

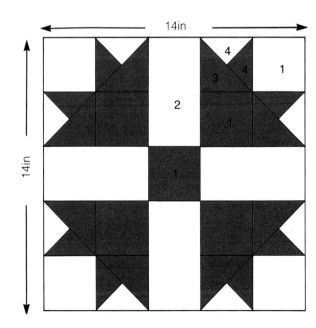

1 cut 4 red dots/4 white/
   1 plain red
2 cut 4 white
3 cut 4 red dots
4 cut 8 red dots/8 white

1 Cut out the fabric pieces accurately with sharp scissors. Pin the pieces with their right sides together, beginning with the smallest (No. 4) triangles. Machine-stitch the pieces together, then stitch to a No. 3 pattern. Make another square like this. Join each to a No. 1 square to make the corner sections. Follow the diagram for color placement.

TIPS

Accuracy in cutting and stitching is essential in patchwork of this type. Cut out carefully using sharp scissors.

Cotton fabrics are generally best. They do not ravel or stretch easily, and they press well.

When joining two pieces, pin at right angles to the seam. This enables you to machine-stitch across the pins without having to baste first.

Open out the seams to prevent bulkiness. Press only very lightly during the early stages; press well from the wrong side when the patchwork is complete.

CUTTING OUT THE FABRIC

From ivory fabric cut:

- 2 pillow backs
- 4 of pattern No. 1
- 4 of pattern No. 2
- 8 of pattern No. 4

From red dotted fabric cut:

- 4 of pattern No. 1
- 4 of pattern No. 3
- 8 of pattern No. 4
- 4 strips $1\frac{1}{2} \times 14\frac{1}{2}$ inches for bindings

From solid red fabric cut:

- 1 of No. 1

2 Stitch two corner sections to a No. 2 pattern as shown. Stitch the remaining No. 2 patterns to the center square, No. 1. Stitch the three sections together to form the pillow front.

3 Press all seams from the wrong side.

4 Machine-stitch a narrow double hem across one long edge of both pillow backs. Pin to the wrong side of the pillow front, matching the raw edges and corners, and overlapping at the center. Pin and machine-stitch the right side of one binding piece to the right side of one pillow edge. The stitching should be ½ inch in from the raw edge. The seam allowance should be trimmed to ¼ inch.

5 Turn the binding to the wrong side, then fold ⅜ inch along the raw edge and pin in place. Slipstitch the folded edge to the original stitching line. Bind the opposite side in the same way.

6 Apply bindings to the remaining two raw edges, tucking in the raw edges at all four corners. Stitch the corners neatly.

Appliqué Wall Hanging

Appliqué is an ancient art. Thousands of years ago, the Egyptians decorated their funeral tents with appliquéd work, and there are examples extant dating as far back as the 19th century B.C. The art was brought to Europe during the Crusades and used to apply coats-of-arms to banners as a symbol to rally troops in battle. Appliqué became an important skill in quiltmaking in later centuries in England and the United States. The "Little School House" motif featured in this wall hanging was a popular design for patchwork quilts during the 19th century. It was usually made from red and white fabric. The geometric shape lends itself well to appliqué work such as this. The main appliqué stitching is done by machine, with the decorative embroidery added by hand.

MATERIALS AND EQUIPMENT

◆ 1½ yards of 44-inch wide ivory cotton fabric

◆ 12 squares (8 × 8 inches) of different patterned red and white cotton fabrics

◆ 8 inches of 44-inch wide red and white gingham fabric for bindings

◆ 1 yard fusible webbing (double-sided adhesive paper for fabric)

◆ tracing paper, pencil, and scissors

◆ sewing needles and pins

◆ matching sewing threads

◆ red stranded embroidery thread

◆ 23½-inch long piece of narrow wooden dowel

1 Trace the Little School House motif. Copy the motif onto the paper side of the fusible webbing in reverse. Cut out a webbing square, leaving about ¾ inch all around the motif. Iron the glue side to the wrong side of each colored fabric square.

Little School House motif – cut 12

cut out unshaded areas

(zigzag-stitch along solid lines)

Heart motif – cut 6

2 Cut out the house shape, then cut out the unshaded areas (refer to the template). Peel off the paper backings and position in the center of the ivory squares. Press each one using a hot iron – the heat will melt the adhesive and fuse the two fabrics together.

3 Thread your sewing machine with red thread and using a ⅛-inch satin-stitch setting, sew over all the raw edges of the patterned motifs. Pull all the loose threads to the wrong side and finish off neatly.

4 Machine-stitch the main squares, right sides together, to make a rectangle three squares across and four squares deep. Press all the seams open from the wrong side.

CUTTING OUT THE FABRIC

From ivory fabric cut:

◆ 1 piece 25 × 33 inches for backing

◆ 12 9 × 9-inch squares

From gingham fabric cut:

◆ 2 strips 1½ × 34¼ inches and strips 1½ × 26½ inches for bindings

◆ 4 rectangles 1½ × 2⅜ inches for hanging loops

5 Using webbing as before, cut out and iron on six small hearts at the points where the seams join. With three strands of red embroidery thread, blanket-stitch around the raw edge and herringbone-stitch over all the seam lines.

6 Machine-stitch the right side of the longer binding pieces to the right side of the hanging, matching the raw edges. Turn the binding to the wrong side, then fold ⅝ inch along the raw edge. Pin and then slipstitch the folded edge to the original stitching line.

7 Apply binding in the same way to the upper and lower edges. Tuck in the raw edges at all four corners, and stitch neatly.

8 Machine-stitch a narrow hem on all four sides of the hanging loop pieces. Slipstitch each piece to the wrong side of the hanging along the upper edge. Slot the wooden dowel through the loops and slip-stitch the open side at each end so that the dowel will not slip out. (The dowel can be removed when the hanging is cleaned.)

Cross-stitch Sampler

Samplers used to be practice pieces for young needlewomen. They were useful study aids – young girls learned their alphabet by embroidering letters; they practiced a whole vocabulary of stitches as they worked; and they built up a repertoire of alphabets and motifs to use in future needlework projects.

Today, samplers are worked purely for decorative purposes. This sampler features the obligatory alphabet and numbers, a "Tree of Life" motif, and brightly colored parrots – not a standard motif in cross-stitch, but a popular Pennsylvanian German motif in the 19th century. Other popular motifs include pineapples (representing hospitality), urns and flowers (symbolizing mourning), houses, and trees. Follow our color scheme, or be creative and design your own using graph paper and colored pencils. You can use the alphabet provided to make your sampler more personal with a name or a commemorative date.

THE ART OF THE NEEDLE

MATERIALS AND EQUIPMENT

◆ 20-inch square of 11-count embroidery canvas

◆ sewing needles, crewel needle, pins

◆ contrasting thread for basting

◆ stranded embroidery silk (refer to chart for colors)

◆ sharp embroidery scissors

1 First locate and mark with a line of basting thread in a contrasting color the center of the canvas, both vertically and horizontally. This will give a reference point from which to begin the embroidery.

2 Cross-stitch is very simple to do. Using only three strands of embroidery thread at a time, work in horizontal rows from right to left.

TIPS

Never cut more than 20 inches of thread at a time, to minimize tangling. Finish off the thread ends neatly on the wrong side as you go.
Count very carefully. Mistakes will throw the pattern out of line. Place marker pins every 10th thread. This will help when counting.

3 Return across the row from left to right, crossing each stitch.

4 Following the color chart, begin at the center, using the basting threads as a guide. This will create a reference point from which to count to the other motifs. From the center, mark every 10th thread with a pin along the basted lines. This will make the counting easier. Work the border in small sections at a time. Continue following the chart until the sampler is complete.

Amish-style Duvet

*Amish quilts are noted for their bold color combinations and simple
geometric patterns — but if you look closely, you see that large
expanses of color are made up of many small squares. Traditionally,
a layer of batting would be sandwiched between the patchwork layer
and the backing piece, and then hand-quilted in intricate patterns,
which sometimes took many weeks or months to complete.
This duvet is based on a traditional Amish design called "Diamond In
A Square," with the central square divided into a nine-patch square. It
is thought to have been inspired by the prayer books the Amish
brought with them to America, which had a central diamond boss and
a boss at each corner. This cover has all the visual impact of a
traditional quilt, but working it involves no hand-quilting. It has a
button opening through which you can insert your comforter.*

1 Begin by piecing small (No. 8) squares at the center, then add on the surrounding border of Nos. 6 and 7 squares. Press each stage lightly, opening the seams where they join another edge. Follow the diagram below to complete the upper layer of the duvet.

Piecing arrangement

MATERIALS AND EQUIPMENT

- ◆ 2 yards of 44-inch wide red cotton fabric
- ◆ 2 yards of 44-inch wide green cotton fabric
- ◆ 2½ yards of 44-inch wide blue cotton fabric
- ◆ 5 yards of 90-inch wide red sheeting fabric (or two sheets)
- ◆ 8 red buttons
- ◆ matching sewing threads
- ◆ scissors
- ◆ sewing needles and pins
- ◆ plain pattern paper
- ◆ pencil
- ◆ ruler and carpenter's square
- ◆ tape measure
- ◆ tailor's chalk

DRAFTING THE PATTERNS

The diagram represents a scale pattern of a
6½ feet square. This will fit a double bed.
Use this diagram to piece together the cover. Trace
on plain paper the smaller pattern pieces, and
mark the larger pieces with tailor's chalk on your
fabric. Use a carpenter's square to check that all the
right angles are accurate.

PATTERN PIECE SIZES AND CUTTING INSTRUCTIONS

All pattern pieces include ⅝-inch seam allowance

Pattern 1: 21-inch square, cut 4 green

Pattern 2: 21 × 40½-inch rectangle, cut 4 blue

Pattern 3: 6-inch square, cut 4 green

Pattern 4: 6 × 30¾-inch rectangle, cut 4 red

Pattern 5: triangle with right-angled edges
measuring 16¾ inches, cut 4 green

Pattern 6: 3⅝-inch square, cut 4 blue

Pattern 7: 3⅝ × 16-inch rectangle, cut 4 red

Pattern 8: 6⅞-inch square, cut 1 blue, 4 red, 4 green

Cut two large squares 80 × 80 inches from the red
sheeting fabric as a lining and a backing for the
duvet.

2 Cut approximately 12 yards of 2¾-inch wide bias strips from the remaining red fabric. Stitch the strips together at right angles to make a continuous bias strip.

3 Baste the lining piece to the wrong side of the upper layer. Pin and stitch the right side of the binding to one edge of the upper piece. Turn the binding to the wrong side, fold ⅝ inch along the raw edge of the binding, then pin and slipstitch the folded edge to the original stitching line. Apply binding to one edge of the backing piece in the same way. Baste the upper layer to the backing piece around the three raw sides.

4 Work 8 buttonholes evenly spaced along the binding of the backing piece. Sew on buttons to correspond on the upper layer. Fasten the opening. Apply bindings to the sides, tuck in the raw edges at the two lower corners. Bind and finish the upper edge in the same way.

Baby Quilt

If you are beginning patchwork, a baby quilt is a good project to start with – it is a manageable size and small enough to be completed quite quickly. This quilt is based on square patterns, from which patchwork was originally made. In this example, six "Evening Star" patchwork squares are joined together and lightly hand-quilted. The "Evening Star" is one of a group of classic star patterns in quilting. This cozy baby quilt is an average crib size, and it makes a light, warm covering – not thick or heavy. Its polyester batting traps the air, keeping the baby warm. Light quilting keeps the batting fluffy, maintaining the insulation – the more hand-quilting you do, the flatter the quilt will become.

Blue star on white

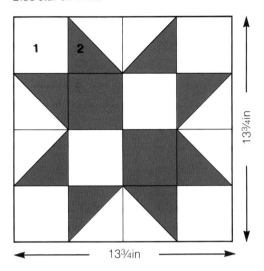

13¾in

13¾in

DRAFTING THE PATTERNS

Using the diagram (above) as a guide, draw a full-size pattern of one star square on plain pattern paper. Cut out pattern pieces 1 and 2. Redraw these pieces adding a ⅝-inch seam allowance to all edges. The quilt is made up of six star squares, three blue stars on white, and three white stars on blue. Follow the larger diagram (right) as a guide to piecing.
Trace the heart-shaped quilting guide.

CUTTING OUT THE FABRIC PIECES

Pattern No. 1 – cut 24 white and 24 blue

Pattern No. 2 – cut 48 white and 48 blue

Cut one 28¾ × 42½-inch rectangle of white for backing

Cut one 28¾ × 42½-inch rectangle of batting

Cut two 5⅛ × 33½-inch strips and two 5 × 47¼-inch strips from ticking for bindings.

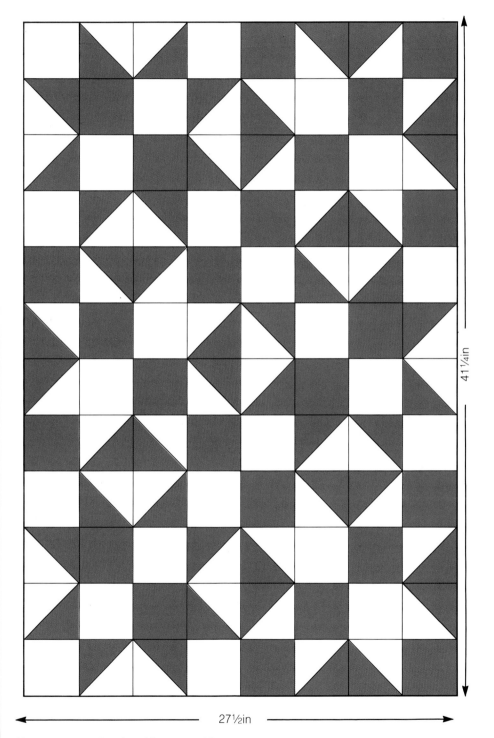

41¼in

27½in

Note: reverse colors for white star on blue

MATERIALS AND EQUIPMENT

- 1¾ yards of 44-inch wide blue checked fabric
- 2¾ yards of 44-inch wide ivory cotton fabric
- 1¼ yards of medium-weight polyester batting
- ¾ yard of 44-inch wide blue and white cotton ticking for binding
  - scissors
  - sewing needles and pins
  - matching sewing thread
  - plain pattern paper
  - pencil

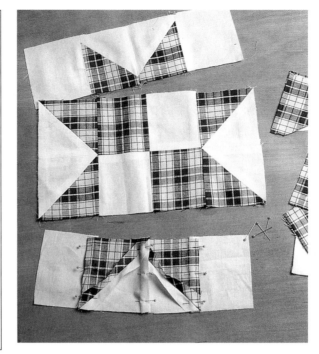

1 Stitch together the four center squares, then join the triangles together in pairs. Join the triangle squares together and stitch to the center panel. Press all seams lightly, pressing them open. Make three blue on white squares and three white on blue squares. Join them together using the large diagram opposite as a guide. Press all seams well from the wrong side.

2 Place the batting between the patchwork layer and the backing fabric. Pin at regular intervals all over the quilt.

3 Using a basting thread in a contrasting color, baste the three layers together. This will prevent slipping during hand-quilting.

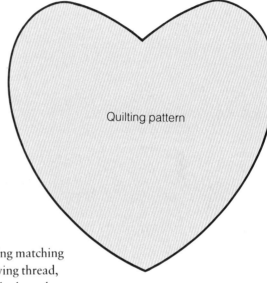

Quilting pattern

4 Using matching sewing thread, hand-quilt along the seam lines between each large square and around the center square panels of each. The quilting stitch is a small running stitch taken through all three layers.

TIP

When hand-quilting, it is better to concentrate on making the stitches even rather than small.

---

5 Pin the heartshaped paper pattern to the plain white squares on the center panel. Hand-quilt around the paper pattern.

6 Stitch the right side of the shorter of the two binding strips to the right side of the quilt, matching the raw edges. Turn the binding to the wrong side and fold ⅝ inch along the raw edge of the binding. Pin and slipstitch the fold to the original stitching line. Apply binding to the other two sides in the same way. Tuck in the raw edges at the four corners and slip-stitch neatly. This will make quite a wide edging.

TIME FOR TOYS

Rag Doll

Checkerboard

Tic-Tac-Toe

Rag Doll

Rag dolls are an old tradition. Their origins are now lost in time and much of their history is unrecorded, but they were probably originally made in poor homes from scraps saved from old clothes to be made into quilts, rugs, and toys. Children still love their rag dolls.

Their attraction is that they are soft and cuddly – and, above all, individual. Every doll is different and has its own character sewn and embroidered into it.

Our rag doll is dressed in cotton and gingham edged with eyelet lace, with ribbon in her hair – but you can use any fabric scraps. The secret of a good doll is in the imaginative use of fabric, notions, and embroidery to give her face a personality.

MATERIALS AND EQUIPMENT

◆ 16 inches of 44-inch wide ivory cotton fabric

◆ 20 inches of 44-inch wide blue gingham fabric

◆ 8 inches blue mini-check gingham fabric

◆ 10 inches of 44-inch wide white cotton poplin

◆ 1¼ yards of narrow white eyelet edging

◆ two squares of navy felt

◆ 8 small blue buttons

◆ 1¼ yards narrow blue satin ribbon

◆ 1 skein bulky knitting yarn for hair

◆ red stranded embroidery thread and scraps of felt for face

◆ 1¼ yards red ribbon for hair bows

◆ scissors

◆ sewing needles and pins

◆ plain pattern paper, pencil, and ruler

◆ fabric glue

◆ matching sewing threads

◆ bag of polyester toy stuffing

DRAFTING THE PATTERNS

Draft full-scale pattern piece using the pattern graph. Follow the cutting instructions and information written on the pattern pieces. Unless otherwise stated, all seam allowances are ⅝ inch and are included in the pattern.

TIME FOR TOYS

place to fold

Doll arm – cut 2 in fabric
(⅝in seam allowance included)

Enlarge the templates
on a photocopier
by 50%

Doll body
– cut 2 in fabric
(⅝in seam allowance
included)

Dress back
– cut 2 in fabric
(⅝in seam allowance
included)

fold here for back opening

place to fold

Doll leg – cut 4 in fabric
(⅝in seam allowance
included)

pin tuck

place to fold

Dress front – cut 1 in fabric
(⅝in seam allowance
included)

¼in hem

fold for casing

Panties – cut 2 in fabric
(⅝in seam allowance
included)

place to fold

place to fold

Apron – cut 1 in fabric
(⅝in seam allowance
included)

Skirt – cut a piece of fabric
29½ × 11in

narrow double hem

fold here for hem

¼in hem

hem

place to fold

Doll boot upper
– cut 2 in felt
(¼in seam allowance
included)

heel

Doll boot sole
– cut 2 in felt
(¼in seam allowance
included)

toe

Boot strap – cut 4 in felt

gather

Sleeve – cut 2 in fabric
(⅝in allowance
included)

place to fold

double hem

1 Machine-stitch the body and limb pieces right sides together as illustrated, leaving open the upper edges of the arm and leg joint, and the lower edges of the body and arm joint. Trim all seam allowances down to ¼ inch and clip into curved seams and to the small dot at the neck.

TIP

Use your imagination to create an individual expression for your doll. Embroider a mouth and glue on two small circles for the eyes.

2 Turn the arms right side out and fill with toy stuffing. Baste across the upper edge, matching the seams. Tuck the stuffed arm inside the body and baste the arm into the arm joint opening, matching the seams at the shoulder and side to the arm seam. Machine-stitch. Attach the other arm in the same way.

3 Turn the body right side out. Turn the legs right side out and stuff with toy filling. Baste across the upper edge, matching the seams. Baste the legs to one side of the lower edge of the doll body. Fill the doll body with toy stuffing and then slipstitch the lower body opening.

4 Cut out two pantie pieces as indicated. Stitch eyelet edging to the lower edge of each leg. Press the seam to the wrong side and topstitch. Machine-stitch the crotch seam together, then stitch the inside leg seam. Press ¼ inch, then 1 inch to the wrong side along the casing edge. Thread the casing with an 8-inch piece of narrow elastic, using a small safety pin. When it is threaded through, stitch the ends of the elastic together securely. Stitch a ribbon bow on each leg and on the front of the casing.

5 **Making the doll's dress** Machine-stitch the tuck down the center front, then fold the center back edge and work the buttonholes where indicated. Stitch the shoulder seams together. Stitch a narrow double hem at the wrist edge of both sleeves, then gather the sleeve cap between the small dots to fit into the armhole. Stitch the sleeves into the armholes, then join the side and sleeve seam in one. Cut an 11 × 29½-inch band for the skirt, stitch the short edges together halfway up the seam. Fold and stitch a hem along the lower edge. Gather the skirt to fit the waist, and machine-stitch in place. Stitch on the buttons to correspond with the buttonholes.

Making the apron Fold and stitch hems where indicated on pattern. Work cross-stitch motifs along lower edge following chart provided. Tack pleats at waist edge then stitch on waistband/tie piece.

6 **The boots** Cut the boot pieces from the felt as indicated. Fold the boot upper in half at the center back and stitch the front seam to the small dot. Fold and stitch a ¼-inch hem along the remainder of the upper edge. Stitch the sole to the upper, positioning the rounded end at the center back. Turn the boots the right side out. Stitch the straps together in pairs very close to the edges. Stitch one end to the boot and attach the other end with a small button.

7 **The hair** Wind the knitting yarn into hanks about 16 inches long. You will need about six hanks for the hair. Wind a length of yarn around your thumb and little finger as shown for the bangs.

8 Stitch the center of the small hank to the forehead for the bangs, then stitch the centers of the other hanks down the back of the head. Tie the yarn in bunches on each side of the head.

Game Boards

Folk art has a fine history of colorful painted boards for games like chess, checkers, and tic-tac-toe. During the 19th century, the decoration of the boards became an art form – many were hung on the walls as decoration when not in use.

The boards that are the theme of the next two projects are inspired by game boards made by amateur painters and sign painters for families on the North American frontier. The boards are easily made from plywood and painted with colorful latex paints.

The checkerboard on the following page has a decorated border – for players to put pieces on when not in play – with a central heart motif and colorful peacocks on each side. The secret of making a game board that looks authentic is to try to use the colors available to painters in the 19th century. Border designs should be painted in shades that mimic the earth pigments used at the time – brick reds, browns, and ochers relieved by olive greens and mellow greenish-blues. The squares should be in darkest brown against parchment or buttermilk shades.

Our tic-tac-toe board which follows has counters made from squares of plywood sanded into smooth shapes. Afterward, you can make a drawstring bag to keep the board and counters together.

Checkerboard

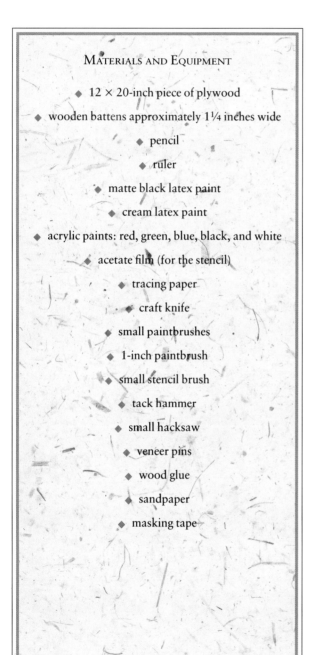

MATERIALS AND EQUIPMENT

- 12 × 20-inch piece of plywood
- wooden battens approximately 1¼ inches wide
- pencil
- ruler
- matte black latex paint
- cream latex paint
- acrylic paints: red, green, blue, black, and white
- acetate film (for the stencil)
- tracing paper
- craft knife
- small paintbrushes
- 1-inch paintbrush
- small stencil brush
- tack hammer
- small hacksaw
- veneer pins
- wood glue
- sandpaper
- masking tape

1 Cut the wooden battens into two 12-inch and two 20-inch lengths. Miter the corners (cut them so that they make a 45° angle) carefully. Glue the frame together, checking the corners with a carpenter's square as you work to make sure that the corners are perfectly square. When the glue is dry, anchor the frame together permanently with veneer pins.

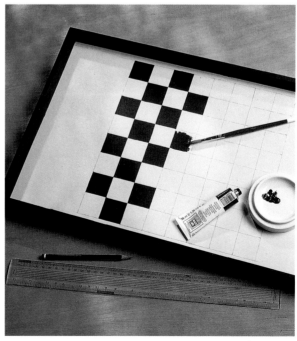

2 Glue and pin the frame to the base. Paint the frame and underside with matte black latex paint, and the face of the board with cream latex paint. Mark the checkerboard grid carefully with a pencil and ruler. Each square must be 1½ × 1½ inches, and the grid must have eight squares along each side. Paint the squares with black acrylic paint using a small brush. Rub away pencil marks with a soft eraser when the paint is completely dry.

Enlarge the
stencil template
on a photocopier
by 25%

3 Trace and enlarge the stencil pattern. Cut a piece of acetate about ¾ inch larger all around than the pattern. Tape the acetate to the tracing and, using a craft knife, carefully cut out the design.

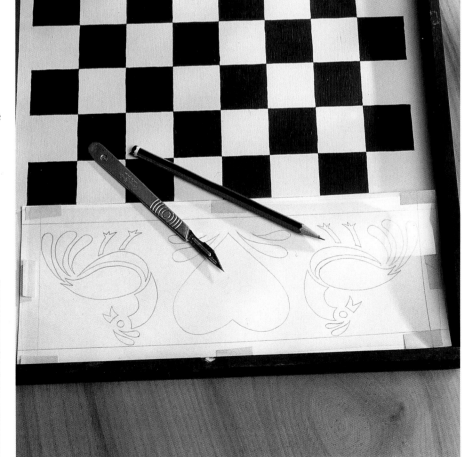

TIP

Acrylic paint are very quick-drying and so are ideal for stenciling. Practice stenciling on a spare sheet of paper before starting to decorate the board. It may take a few trial runs to get the colors and technique right.

4 Tape the stencil to the checkerboard. Mix the colors you need in a palette, to quite a thick consistency. Apply the paint sparingly with a stencil brush and a dabbing motion. Apply one color at a time and cover any areas you want to leave unpainted with masking tape. Allow each color to dry before applying the next. Peel off the stencil and repeat the process on the other end of the board.

5 Paint in finer details with a small brush, using the picture opposite as a guide.

Tic-Tac-Toe

TIP

To sand the counters, lay the sandpaper on your work surface and drag the edge of the counter along it until the corner is rounded.

1 Cut the wooden edging into four 4½-inch pieces. Butt the pieces together to fit the base. Glue and pin the frame.

2 Glue and pin the frame to the square base. Paint the frame and underside with matte black latex paint, and the face of the board with cream.

3 Cut nine square pieces from the 1¼-inch-wide wooden batten, then sand the edges to smooth curves.

4 Paint each counter with matte black latex paint, then paint 0s on one side and Xs on the other with white acrylic paint.

WELCOME HOME

Candles

Herbal Hot Plate and Sachets

Festive Garlands

Painted Chest

Candles

Candlelight has a soft, golden glow that spreads an atmosphere of serenity across a table or around a room. The mustard-buff shade of beeswax enhances the warmth of the light from candles made from natural wax – candlemakers add some beeswax to paraffin wax to give composition candles a natural color.

You can make your own candles very simply from hand-rolled sheets of the beeswax used by beekeepers to line the hives as a base for the bees to build their honeycombs. You can cut the sheets into strips to make straight-sided candles, or triangles which, when rolled, make elegant tapered candles. The beeswax sheets are imprinted with a hexagonal honeycomb pattern which gives the finished candles a decorative surface texture. When lit, the beeswax burns with a lovely fragrance.

1 **Tapered candles** Cut the beeswax sheet in half diagonally using a craft knife and a metal ruler.

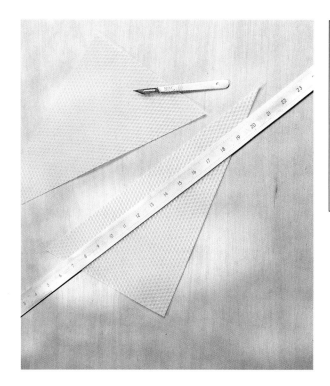

2 Cut a length of wick ¾ inch longer than the candle. Roll the edge of the beeswax sheet around the wick quite tightly, so that the wick is held firmly in place, then roll toward the tapered end, keeping the lower straight edge level. The beeswax sticks to itself.

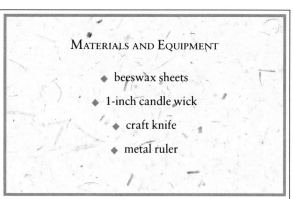

MATERIALS AND EQUIPMENT

◆ beeswax sheets

◆ 1-inch candle wick

◆ craft knife

◆ metal ruler

3 **Straight-sided candles** For straight-sided candles, cut the sheet into straight strips.

Herbal Hot Plate and Sachets

In the past, herbs had many practical uses around the house. The scent of lavender and other herbs kept insects away, so these would be sprinkled on floors and under rugs, and hung from the rafters as an insect-repellent as well as an air freshener. "Washing herbs" would be added to the water in which bedlinen was washed to discourage bugs, and lavender was sewn into sachets, which would be placed among the folds of clothes stored in drawers and chests as moth-proofing. The sachets were made from scraps of cheesecloth and other loose-woven fabrics that would let the scent of the herbs seep through.

Dry your own herbs and flowers to make fragrant and colorful decorations for your home – bunches of herbs tied with fabric bows for the kitchen, and lavender sachets for the wardrobe. Or fill a pretty fabric pouch with bay leaves and cloves to use instead of a trivet – the warmth of the dish will release the scent of the herbs inside.

- ◆ selection of fresh herbs and flowers (sage, bay, marjoram, lavender)
- ◆ cloves
- ◆ two 10-inch squares of lightweight, loosely woven fabric for the hot plate
- ◆ assorted ribbons and fabric strips
- ◆ thick cotton embroidery thread for tie-quilting
- ◆ sharp needle, tapestry needle, and pins
- ◆ scissors and pencil

TIP

To make lavender hearts, stitch two fabric heart shapes right sides together, leaving a small gap in the stitching. Turn right side out. Fill with lavender. Slipstitch over the gap. Stitch on a ribbon bow and a hanging loop.

1 Drying herbs and flowers Preheat your oven to about 150°. Tie the herbs or flowers loosely in small bunches, then arrange on a baking sheet with a space between each bunch. Place in the oven for about 45 minutes. Remove from the oven and allow to cool. Tie the bunches with pretty ribbons or fabric strips, or snip off the stems and remove the leaves with your hands for pot stands, sachets, and other uses.

Alternatively, you can tie the fresh herbs or flowers in bundles and hang them upside-down in a warm place to let them dry naturally. This may take several days.

2 **Hot plate** Stitch the two 10-inch squares together leaving a 1½-inch gap in the stitching on one side. Trim diagonally across each corner.

3 Turn the bag right side out and fill with dried bay leaves, herbs, and cloves. Slipstitch to close the gap.

4 Using a tapestry needle and a double length of embroidery thread, pass the needle from the front through to the back and then to the front again. Tie the threads securely in a knot and finish the ends.

Festive Garlands

Garlands turn an occasion into a festival, and they are the perfect ornament for seasonal festivities, from Easter to Christmas. There are countless ways to adapt a basic garland design to make it appropriate for any seasonal event. An Advent ring decorated with dried flowers is easily converted into a spring garland with ivy and clematis.

Our unusual vine garland is designed for a harvest festival or an outdoor party in the fall. It is entwined with vine leaves, hung with green and red grapes, and finished with roses. In France's Champagne region, many vine-growers plant bright red roses at the ends of the rows of vines. The blooms help the growers make a simple red-green color vision test for an early warning of vine disease — if the vines are sickly, the different shade of green will be immediately apparent in contrast to the red of the roses. Our vine garland would look pretty hanging on a door or a gate post, hung on an outside wall — or perhaps a vine plant — or laid on a picnic table.

1 Choose long, supple stems of vines or other climbing plants, such as clematis, that can be entwined around the ring. The stems must be in full leaf.

MATERIALS AND EQUIPMENT

◆ twisted twig-ring; ours was 11¾in in diameter

◆ stub wires

◆ wire cutters

◆ flower scissors or secateurs

◆ trails of vine leaves

◆ bunches of black and white grapes

◆ roses

2 Cut a stub wire in half and bend it to make a U-shaped staple. Place a stem over the ring and, where possible, push the stem end under the twig-ring binding. Attach the trailing stem to the twig-ring with a wire staple. Continue attaching stems to the ring until it is covered with stems and leaves.

3 Cut the grapes into small but dense bunches that will make the ring look abundant. Position the grapes over the ring so they will hang down in a natural-looking way. Attach them to the ring by hooking a stub wire staple over the stem and into the ring.

TIP

Put the roses next to the red grapes, which will bring out their color.

4 Attach the roses to one side of the ring (at about 11 o'clock) by threading the stems under the twig-ring binding.

Painted Chest

The samplers and quilts young girls used to make each year were stored in hope chests, ready for use when, as young women, they married. Solidly made of carved and decorated wood, the hope chest would be as large and impressive as the family could afford – the wealthier the family, the bigger and more magnificent the chest. Traditionally, hope chests were decorated with panels painted with the names of the owner and her family, and symbolic images such as unicorns, considered guardians of virginity. Later the husband's name would be added.

This project is a traditional chest design that you can use to decorate a wooden chest of any size. Our design was inspired by the "Star and Heart" appliqué motifs on a quilt made in 1875.

1 First sand the chest to remove any old paint or varnish and to key the surface ready for painting. Wipe away dust with a soft cloth soaked in mineral spirits. Apply two coats of blue latex paint. Allow each to dry. Trace the central motif and corner stars from the templates on page 106. You may need to extend the joining motif to fit the space on your chest. Tape the traced motifs to squares of chalk-backed carbon paper of the same size.

2 Tape the paper patterns to the chest, positioning them carefully. Transfer the designs to the painted surface by tracing through the layers with a pencil.

MATERIALS AND EQUIPMENT

- ◆ wooden chest
- ◆ sandpaper
- ◆ blue latex paint
- ◆ acrylic paints: yellow and red
- ◆ small paintbrush
- ◆ mixing palette
- ◆ 2-inch paintbrush
- ◆ tracing paper
- ◆ pencil
- ◆ ruler
- ◆ chalk-backed carbon paper
- ◆ masking tape
- ◆ soft cloth
- ◆ mineral spirits

Joining motif
(extend to correct size)

corner motif – edge

main motif

3 Using a small paintbrush and red acrylic paint, carefully fill in the red areas of the design.

4 Allow the first painted sections to dry, then fill in the yellow areas. When the paint is dry, wipe the surface with a soft cloth soaked in mineral spirits to remove any remaining chalk marks.

CELEBRATIONS

Christmas Decorations

Heart and Hand Greeting Cards

Cut-Paper Projects

Fractur

Christmas Decorations

*Evergreen branches and berries of holly, ivy, bay, and mistletoe have
for centuries been used to decorate houses at Christmas in addition to
the appealing sight of festive foods and lights. The Christmas tree itself
is of course a universal symbol of Christmas and is central to the
festivities in most homes.*

*Nowadays, an enormous and elaborate selection of glass, metal, tinsel,
and wooden decorations can be purchased, but there is no need to buy
expensive Christmas tree decorations. Ornaments you make yourself
are always much more original and satisfying. Here are some ideas for
decorations to make for Christmas and other celebrations, from
colorful scraps of fabric and ribbon, natural raffia, even brown paper,
and pieces of shiny tin.*

MATERIALS AND EQUIPMENT

- ◆ old tin cans (remove the lid and base and open the side piece)
- ◆ tin snips
- ◆ center punch, tack hammer
- ◆ fabric scraps
- ◆ brown paper
- ◆ natural raffia
- ◆ ribbons
- ◆ thick cotton embroidery thread
- ◆ bodkin
- ◆ sewing needle and pins
- ◆ scissors
- ◆ tracing paper
- ◆ pencil
- ◆ hole punch
- ◆ pinking shears
- ◆ toy stuffing
- ◆ double-sided tape
- ◆ masking tape

TIP

Wear protective gloves when cutting the tin.

1 **Tin decorations**
Trace the pattern. Cut the basic shape from the tin with tin snips.

2 Tape the paper tracing to the tin shape. Punch along the pattern lines using the center punch and a tack hammer. Tie on a ribbon hanging loop.

3 **Paper decorations**
Trace the pattern. Cut out shapes from brown paper with pinking shears. Punch a row of small holes around each one, about ⅜ inch in from the edge, using a hole punch.

4 Stitch around the edge using thick embroidery thread and a bodkin. Attach a raffia bow and a hanging loop with double-sided tape.

Fabric

Paper

Fabric

Paper

Fabric

Paper

5 **Fabric decorations**
Trace the pattern. Cut two fabric pieces. Machine- or hand-stitch the pieces, right sides together, ⅝ inch from the raw edge. Leave a 1¼-inch gap in the stitching on one side. Trim the seam allowance to ¼ inch.

6 Turn the shape right side out and press. Machine-stitch about ¼ inch from the edge, leaving the 1¼-inch gap free. Fill lightly with toy stuffing. Stitch over the gap and sew on a ribbon bow and a hanging loop.

Heart and Hand Greeting Cards

*When paper, colorings, and pretty fabrics like satin and lace were
expensive and hard to come by, tokens of greeting were keepsakes to
be treasured for a lifetime. Even today, people appreciate the thought
and care that goes into designing and making a card for an important
occasion — a birthday, the birth of a child, an anniversary.
A beautifully made card is a keepsake, today as always. Our greeting
card of woven paper bears a symbolic heart and hand. A heart always
signifies love or romance, and it is believed that a hand-shaped card
harks back to an old English tradition of giving a glove to a lady as a
token of affection on St. Valentine's day — because the word rhymes
with the word "love."*

CELEBRATIONS

Templates for heart and hand card

Templates for heart card

1 Trace the template. Cut out the heart, hand, and wristband with scissors. Make the diagonal cuts with a craft knife and ruler.

2 Thread the band through the slots at the wrist. With the heart shape pointing toward the fingers, begin weaving the two pieces together. Tuck 2 under A, 3 under B, 4 under C, and so on. Push the heart shape up toward the fingers. Lift A and bring Point 3 up over the top. Weave 4 over B and tuck under A.

TIP

Mark the numbers and letters on the cardboard lightly with pencil to avoid confusion. Use the other templates to make smaller cards, the weaving method is the same.

3 Weave 5 over C, under B, then bring it out on top of A. Weave 6 over D, under C, over B, then tuck the point under A. Continue in this way to form the pattern.

4 Tuck all the numbered points in at the center.

Cut-Paper Projects

From China and Japan to the Middle East, Mexico and the Balkan countries, cut-paper designs have been a folk art for centuries. In eastern Europe, peasants and farm workers hung paper-cutting "curtains" in the windows of their houses and decorated the walls with cut-out paper patterns. Their intricate designs were made to keep, and appreciated as art, not throwaway decoration.

This heart-shaped cutout, surrounded by tulips, is inspired by the delicate cut-paper work of a 19th-century Swiss woodcutter, Johan Hauswirth. Simple positive and negative effects are created by first folding a paper square into quarters, then cutting out a simple motif inspired by a design taken from an old Hawaiian appliqué quilt.

1 Fold an 8¾-inch square of paper into quarters, then trace the design of the folded paper motif onto it. Cut around the traced design with sharp scissors.

2 Open out the paper and glue it to a sheet of paper in a contrasting color.

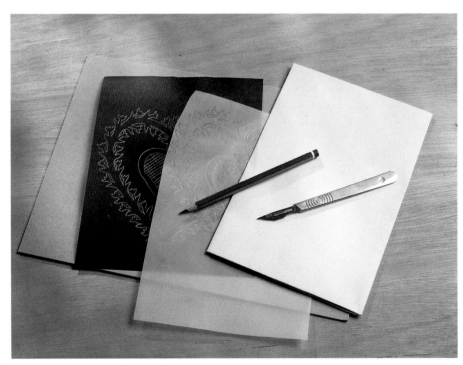

MATERIALS AND EQUIPMENT

◆ black- and cream-colored paper and cardboard

◆ tracing paper

◆ pencil

◆ scissors

◆ craft knife

◆ masking tape

◆ paper glue

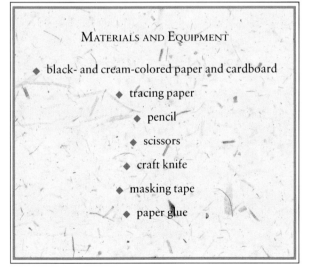

3 Trace the design of the motif. Transfer it to black paper using chalk-backed carbon paper.

4 Cut away the main surplus areas with scissors, then work into the more detailed parts with a craft knife. Glue the finished cutout to a piece of cardboard in a contrasting color.

Cut paper motif

Folded paper motif

place to folded edge

place to folded edge

Fractur

The old art of Fractur practiced by German settlers in North America has special relevance today, as the art of calligraphy is regaining popularity. A Fractur was a document – a record of some important anniversary or other event, written by a calligrapher who copied the details in a script similar to that used in medieval illuminated manuscripts (the German word Fractur means "broken script"). Pennsylvanian settlers developed Fractur into a folk art form, decorating their commemorative scripts with drawings, motifs, and mottoes. Hearts were often a central feature, surrounded by floral designs, and birds and animals were popular. Our design uses a traditional central heart bordered by tulips. You can substitute gothic or italic script for the Fractur if you find it easier.

1 Trace the design, then transfer the design lines and calligraphy guide to the sheet of handmade paper. Now write the message. You may need to practice writing with the calligraphy pen on a spare sheet of paper.

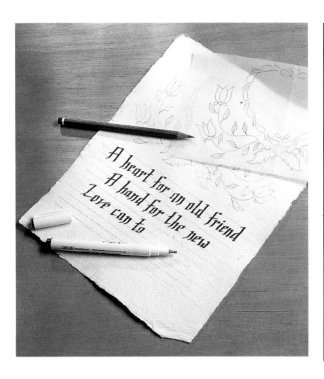

MATERIALS AND EQUIPMENT

◆ 8 × 10¼-inch sheet of handmade paper

◆ acrylic paints: red, blue, green, yellow

◆ small paintbrushes

◆ tracing paper

◆ pencil

◆ ruler

◆ 2mm calligraphy pen

◆ colored background paper

◆ picture frame

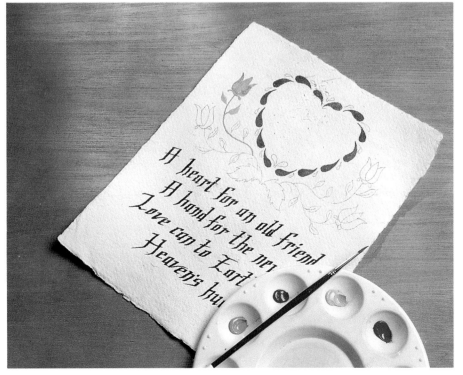

2 Paint in the colored design using acrylic paints and a small paintbrush.

TIP

We used a small sheet of handmade paper because it had a nice deckle edge. You could use a larger sheet of paper and tear the edge carefully to create the same effect.

A heart for an old friend
A hand for the new
Love can to earth lend
Heaven's hue

3 Mount the fractur on contrasting colored paper or fabric and then frame it. Write sayings, commemorative dates, or greetings. This can make a really beautiful and personal gift for a special occasion.

INDEX